CLEVER MACHINERY

JOHN ALLAN

Contents

1. MACHINES

Amazing Machines — 4

Marvellous Machinery — 6

2. WHEELS AND RAMPS

Roller Coasters — 8

3. PULLEYS AND LEVERS

Up and Down — 10

4. PROPULSION

Over the Hill — 12

Magnetic Propulsion — 14

Catapult Launch — 16

5. MATERIALS

Wooden Roller Coasters — 18

Steel Roller Coasters — 20

6. STRONG STRUCTURES

Fantastic Structures — 22

Strong Shapes — 24

7. DESIGN

Creating New Rides — 26

8. NEW TECHNOLOGY

The Future — 28

Glossary — 30

Index — 32

Amazing Machines

A roller coaster travels at amazing speeds, to dizzying heights, with exciting twists and turns. But, a roller coaster is still just a machine.

AMAZING MACHINES

Machines are all around us. We use them every day. Some are simple and some are complex. Wheels, levers and scissors are all simple.

Complex machines include mechanical watches, helicopters, and electric cars. A simple machine has one of four basic components: wheel, **ramp**, **pulley**, and **lever.** All machines contain at least one of these things. While most machines are tools that make our lives easier, some machines are built just for fun—like roller coasters.

A loop the loop on a roller coaster. The wheels and track are parts of an exciting machine.

THAT'S AMAZING!

Your muscles and bones form a natural machine—your body! This allows you to move.

Marvellous Machinery

Machines

WHAT IS A MACHINE?

A machine is a device that acts on another object. It might help you push or move something. People use machines to make a task easier. For example, a bicycle lets you move quickly with little effort.

SIMPLE AND COMPLEX MACHINES

A bottle opener is a very simple machine. It has no moving parts. Most machines, though, have many moving parts. The parts of a machine interact with each other to do work.

A complex machine such as a theme park ride often contains a number of smaller, simple machines. For example, an engine may contain many moving parts that act as wheels and levers. These simple machines make the engine run.

The world's first tubular steel roller coaster was The Matterhorn Bobsleds in Disneyland, California, USA. It opened in 1959 and Walt Disney had the idea after a trip he made to the Swiss Alps.

The **axle** goes through the center of this big wheel. The wheel rotates around the axle and is a simple machine.

Roller Coasters
Wheels and Ramps

Roller coasters use two basic types of simple machines—wheels and ramps. Wheels make the cars move. Ramps help the cars gain or lose height.

WHAT ARE WHEELS AND RAMPS?

Our everyday lives depend upon the wheel. Without it, we would have no easy way to transport objects or ourselves around. A wheel turning around a fixed **axle** is a simple machine.

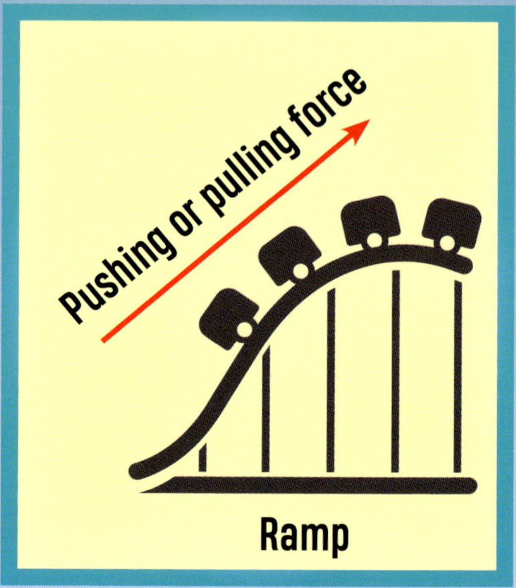

A ramp is another simple and useful machine. We use ramps all the time without realising it.

A ramp is simply a slope, or **inclined plane**. Ramps allow us to raise or lower objects more easily.

ROLLER COASTER MACHINE

With some help from **gravity** and other **forces**, roller coasters deliver a thrilling ride! Gravity pulls all objects toward Earth. The force of gravity also makes objects **accelerate** as they fall to the ground.

Roller coasters are machines made of ramps and wheels.

Gravity is about to pull this roller coaster down a slope. Its wheels allow a smooth ride at super-fast speeds.

Up and Down
Pulleys and Levers

Pulleys and levers are two types of simple machines. Pulleys change the direction in which a force pulls. Levers use a *pivot* point to help move an object. A seesaw is a common example of a lever.

Pulling down on one end of the rope lifts up the weight on the other end of the rope.

WHAT IS A PULLEY?

A wheel and rope make up a simple machine called a pulley. The rope loops around the wheel to make it turn. Pulling one end of the rope turns the wheel. This pulls on an object attached to the other end of the rope. Some roller coasters use pulleys to pull the cars up the first hill.

THAT'S AMAZING!

X-scream in Las Vegas, USA, is a seesaw ride over the edge of the Stratosphere Tower, 305 metres above the ground!

PIVOT IN THE CENTRE OF LEVER

Pivot

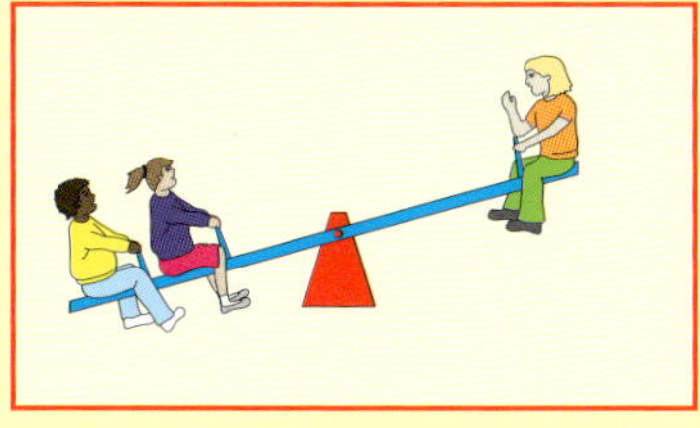

The weight of the two children pushes up the child at the other end.

PIVOT OFF-CENTRE

Pivot

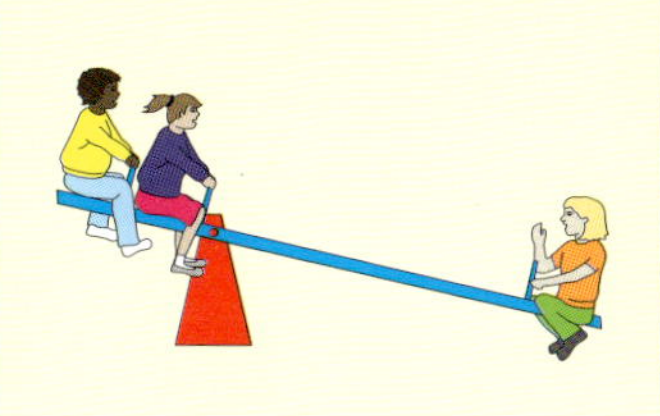

By moving the pivot point, the weight of one child is enough to push up the heavier weight of two children.

WHAT IS A LEVER?

A lever is a long bar that uses a pivot point. As one end is pushed down, the other end gets pushed up. The pivot point of a lever is not always in the middle. It can be at any point along the bar, including at either end.

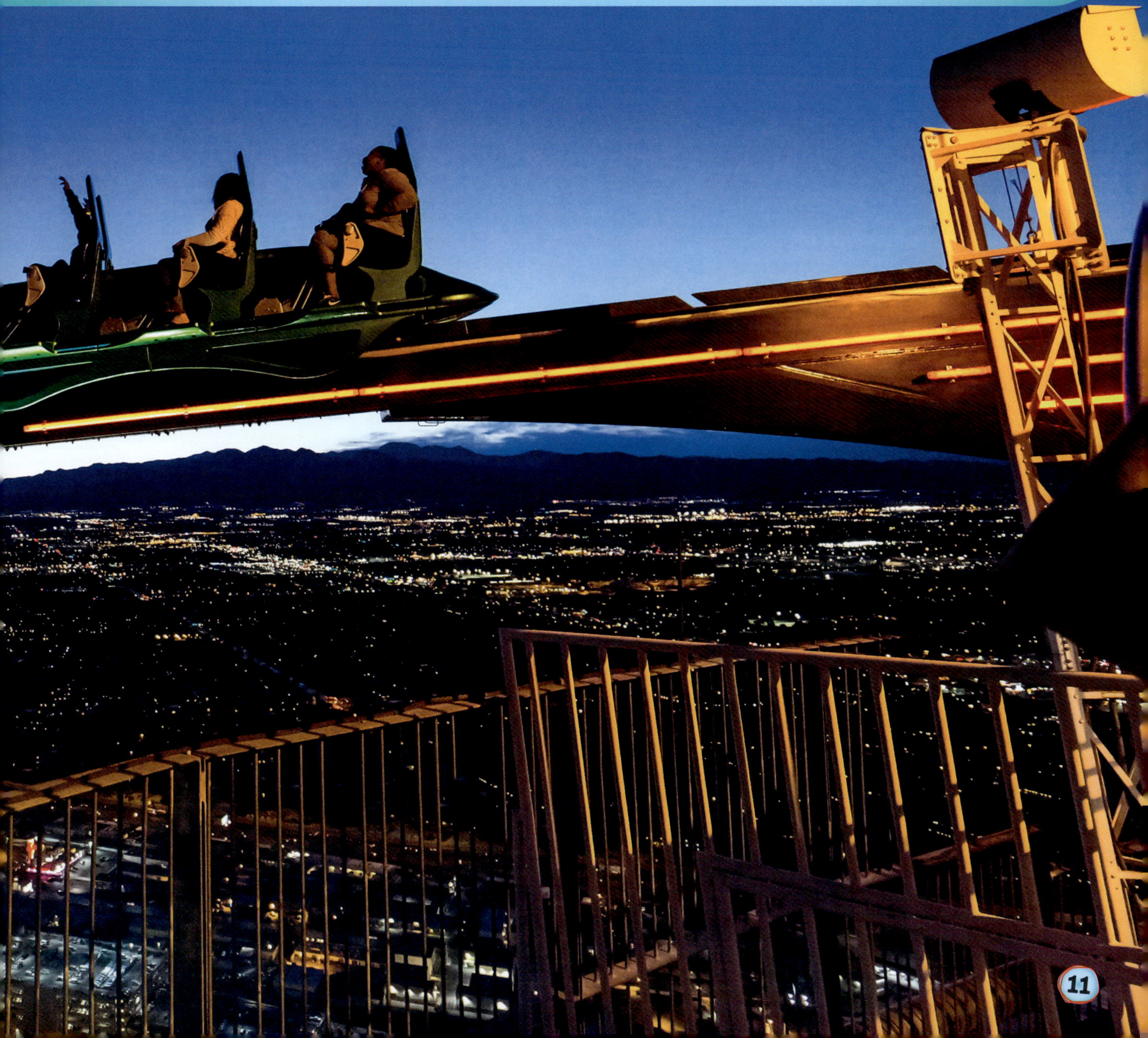

Over the Hill
Propulsion

There are two ways to propel, or move, a roller coaster. One way is to pull it to the top of a hill. Another way is to **catapult** it into motion from a standstill.

GRAVITATIONAL PROPULSION

Many roller coasters use gravity to propel them. A **chain lift** pulls the cars to the top of the first—and tallest—**lift hill**. Then gravity takes over. The **weight** of the cars helps pull the cars down, and the fun begins!

ROLLER COASTERS AND AUTOMOBILES

Roller coaster cars and automobiles can both travel fast, but they are propelled in very different ways. Automobiles have engines that provide power. Roller coaster cars have no engine. They cannot move by themselves. A separate source of power must propel a roller coaster car.

A roller coaster is pulled up the lift hill to the top ...

Roller coaster Baron in the Netherlands, just before a 30 metre vertical drop

... then gravity will propel it down the hill and through the ride.

Magnetic Propulsion

Propulsion

LAUNCHED COASTERS

Some modern roller coasters are not pulled up a lift hill to be released. They are launched from the starting station, often shooting straight up a hill. These are called launched coasters.

One type of launch system uses **magnetic propulsion.** It works by using huge **electromagnets** fitted into the tracks and beneath the cars. It then changes the magnetic **poles** quickly to **attract** and **repel** the cars. This accelerates the cars around the tracks.

HOW MAGNETS WORK

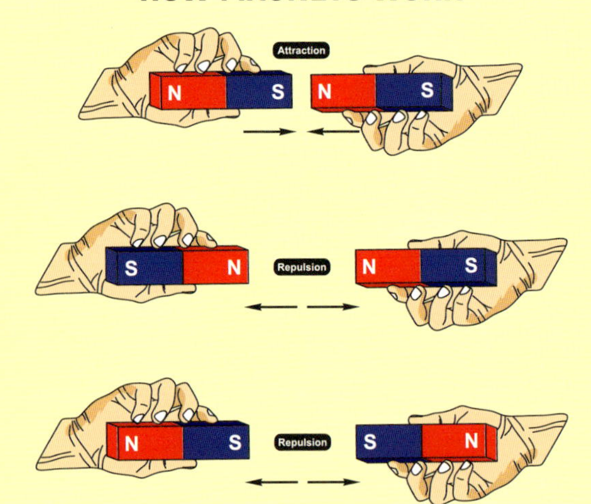

If the cars' **magnets** are N (north) and the track's magnets are S (south) they will be attracted (pulled together).

If the cars' magnets are N (north) and the track's magnets are also N (north) then they will be repelled (pushed apart).

The launch starts with the magnets on the track changing their poles to those opposite the cars' magnets. For example, the cars are south so the track becomes north. This attracts the cars forward. Then, once the cars reach that set of magnets, they change poles, repelling the cars toward the next set of magnets.

Red Force, in Spain is a high-speed accelerator coaster using magnets to propel the cars. It reaches an incredible 62 mph in 2 seconds and 110 mph in 5 seconds. It's the fastest roller coaster in Europe!

Catapult Launch
Propulsion

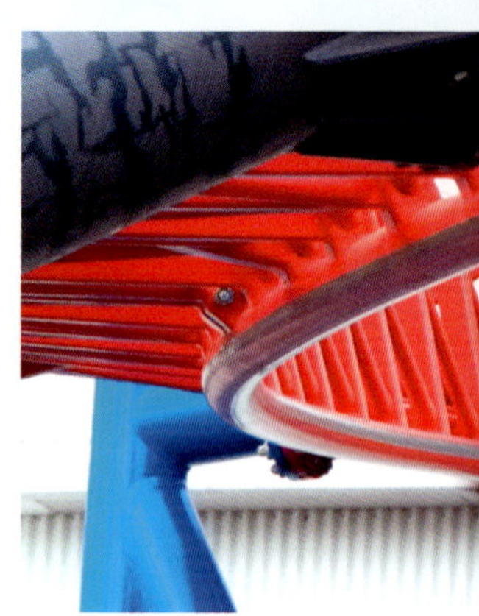

HYDRAULIC LAUNCHES

Instead of slowly moving up that first hill, some roller coasters catapult the cars from a dead start. A catapult launch releases a huge burst of **energy** to propel the cars up the hill at great speed.

There are not many roller coasters that use this system at the moment. Superman in Australia, and Storm Runner and Hypersonic XLC in the USA are three examples.

The hydraulics provide the power to launch the ride. Riders accelerate with such force that their bodies can feel up to five times heavier than normal!

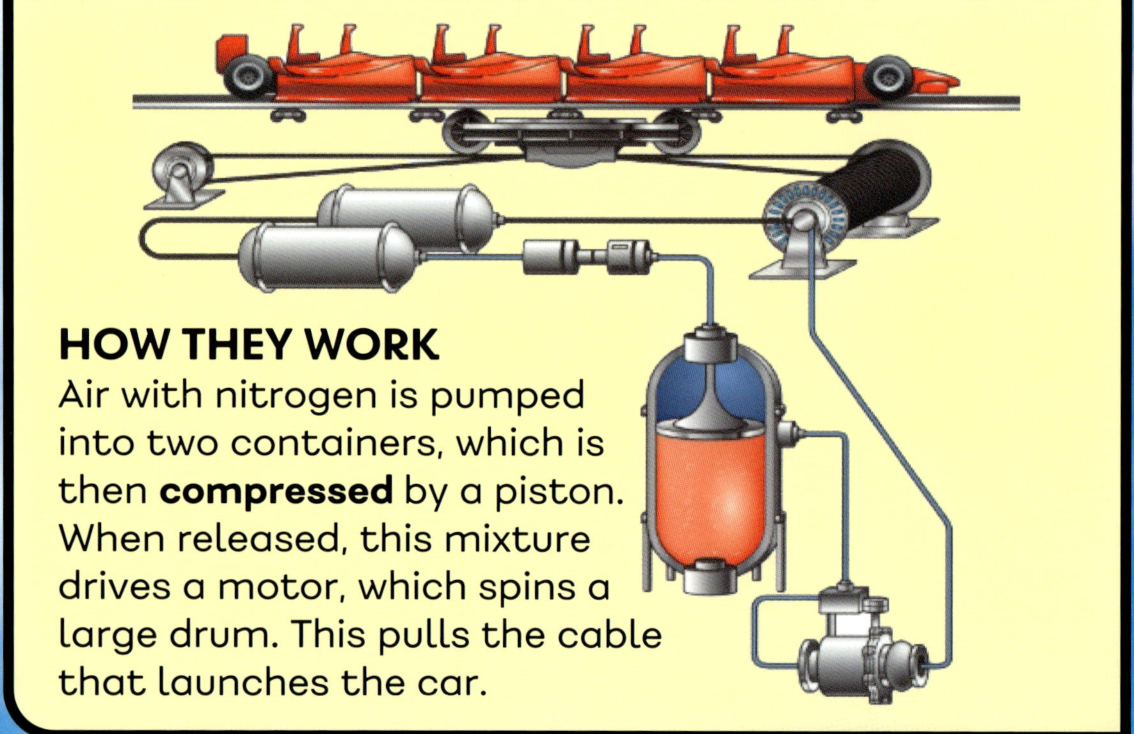

HOW THEY WORK

Air with nitrogen is pumped into two containers, which is then **compressed** by a piston. When released, this mixture drives a motor, which spins a large drum. This pulls the cable that launches the car.

Superman in Australia, starts in a fake subway station. The ground tremors and the coaster launches out of the wall into its thrilling ride.

Hypersonic XLC in Virginia, USA launches riders from 0-79 mph in 1.8 seconds!

Superman reaches speeds of 62 mph to a height of 40 metres. The ride takes thrill-seekers over a top hat, round a steeped bank, passing through a second station and over a camel hump. Then it sweeps under a very low bar, called a "headchopper", as the riders feel as though it will hit them in the head! Of course, the bar is several feet above them.

Wooden Roller Coasters

Materials

Roller coasters have frames made either of wood or steel. Each material provides a thrilling but unique ride. Wooden and steel frames react differently as the roller coaster cars roar over them.

WOODEN ROLLER COASTERS

Roller coaster builders have used wooden frames for more than one hundred years. Wooden beams bolted together form a strong but flexible framework.

PROPERTIES OF WOOD
Wood is a great material for roller coaster structures. It is lighter than steel but still quite strong. It flexes (bends) and sways slightly as the cars roll along. Wooden-framed roller coasters rattle and shake. Many roller coaster fans enjoy this feeling!

Steel Roller Coasters

Materials

Many roller coaster frames are now built completely from steel. Their tracks are steel tubes joined to steel supports. This design allows for a smoother ride. Unlike wood, the steel frame does not move as the riders fly through incredible twists and loop the loops.

PROPERTIES OF STEEL

Steel is an ideal material for building roller coasters. It is very strong and can be molded into any shape. Long, curving sections welded together form **rigid** structures to provide a ride with sharp twists and turns.

DID YOU KNOW?

A typical steel roller coaster like The Big One in Blackpool, UK, contains 2,442 tons of steel. Sixty thousand bolts hold it together.

Fantastic Structures

Strong Structures

The structure that supports a roller coaster is built using common construction methods. It consists of a series of vertical, horizontal, and crossbeam supports.

Wooden roller coaster frames have **intricate** designs. Vertical (up-and-down) supports hold up the tracks. In between them, a lattice (an open pattern) of sideways and diagonal crossbeams strengthen the structure.

SUPPORTING LOADS

The load on a structure is the force that it must withstand without breaking. Most structures only need to support the weight of their materials. Roller coaster frameworks must also withstand additional forces as riders and cars thunder around the tracks.

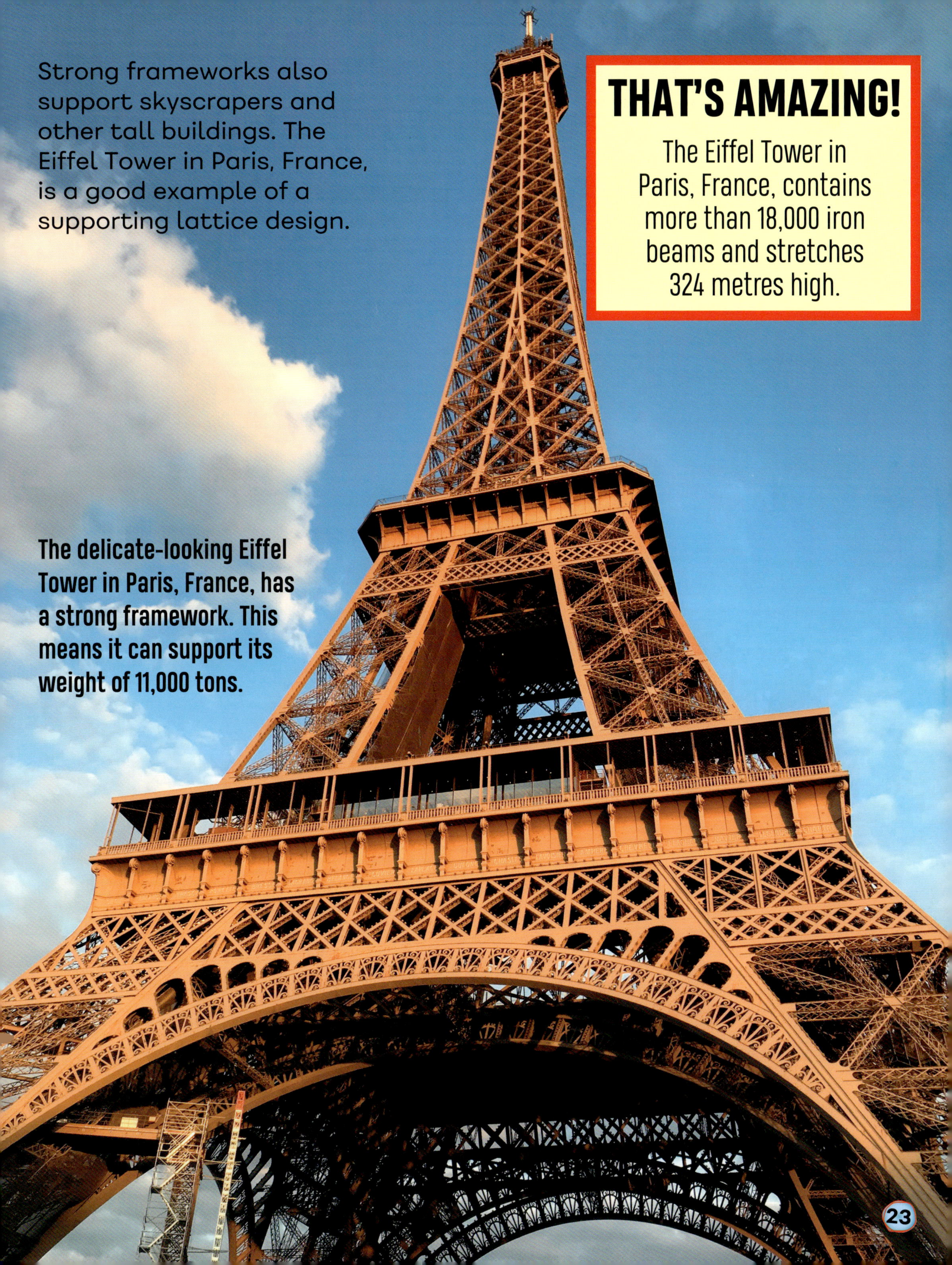

Strong frameworks also support skyscrapers and other tall buildings. The Eiffel Tower in Paris, France, is a good example of a supporting lattice design.

THAT'S AMAZING!
The Eiffel Tower in Paris, France, contains more than 18,000 iron beams and stretches 324 metres high.

The delicate-looking Eiffel Tower in Paris, France, has a strong framework. This means it can support its weight of 11,000 tons.

Strong Shapes
Strong Structures

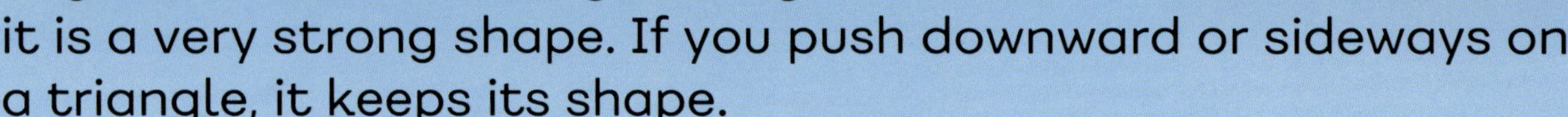

Most roller coaster frames have crossbeams and supports that often form triangles. Engineers use the triangle design because it is a very strong shape. If you push downward or sideways on a triangle, it keeps its shape.

A square is a weak shape compared to a triangle. A sideways force pushing on a square will usually squash it flat. A diagonal support or crossbeam strengthens a square shape because the square has become two triangles!

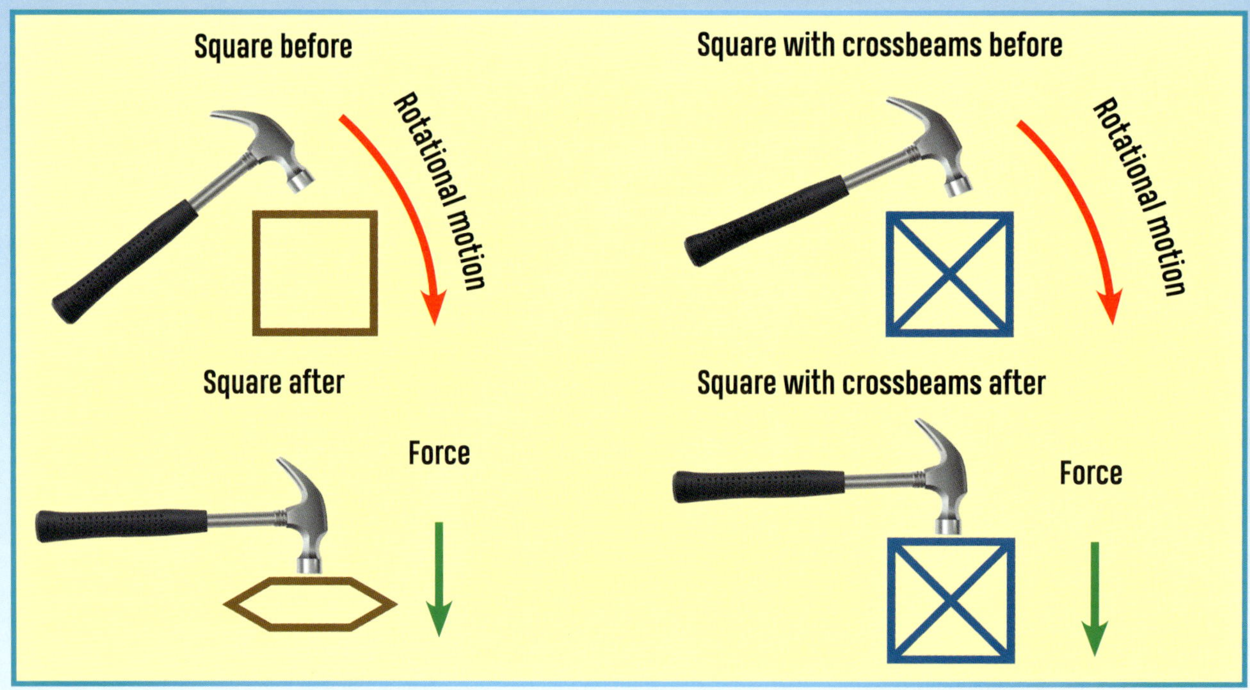

STEEL STRUCTURES

Like a triangle, a tube is another strong shape used in construction. The tube shape also helps to reduce the weight of the material. So instead of solid steel pipes, a roller coaster frame is often made of hollow steel tubes.

THAT'S AMAZING!

The Spaceship Earth dome at The Epcot Center, Florida, USA is a shape called a **geodesic dome**. It is made from 11,324 triangles.

Creating New Rides
Design

Some roller coaster riders prefer smooth rides. Others seek out a jolting, edge-of-their-seat experience. Design engineers create their roller coaster layouts to give riders maximum thrills. Every roller coaster has its own unique design.

DESIGNED TO THRILL

Designers must think about who will ride their machine. Roller coasters designed for small children should have gentle hills and slow cars. Thrill seekers prefer dizzying heights, sharp turns, and incredible speeds.

The designers know exactly how to make their rides more exciting. The first drop is usually the steepest and most terrifying. It catches riders by surprise. Low "head chopper" bars are another scary design trick. They are placed so it seems they just miss hitting riders' heads.

DID YOU KNOW?
Most roller coasters are designed using a computer. That way, the designers can take virtual rides themselves!

The Future
New Technology

Thrill engineers create new and exciting rides. Science, engineering, and maths are all needed to build these multi-million dollar machines.

HIGH-TECH ADVANCES

Technology is advancing at a dizzying rate. Electromagnetic propulsion will fire thrill seekers at even faster speeds. Mighty coasters over 70 metres with vertical drop will soon be the norm.

At Nickelodeon Universe, an exciting new indoor theme park in New Jersey, US, there is a roller coaster that bursts through the roof into a see-through tower to view the Manhattan skyline, before banking into a 121 degree drop. It has become the steepest coaster in the world!

DID YOU KNOW?

The name for a new, 150 metre high, roller coaster in Florida has not yet been decided. Possible choices are "Atmocoaster" and "Teracoaster."

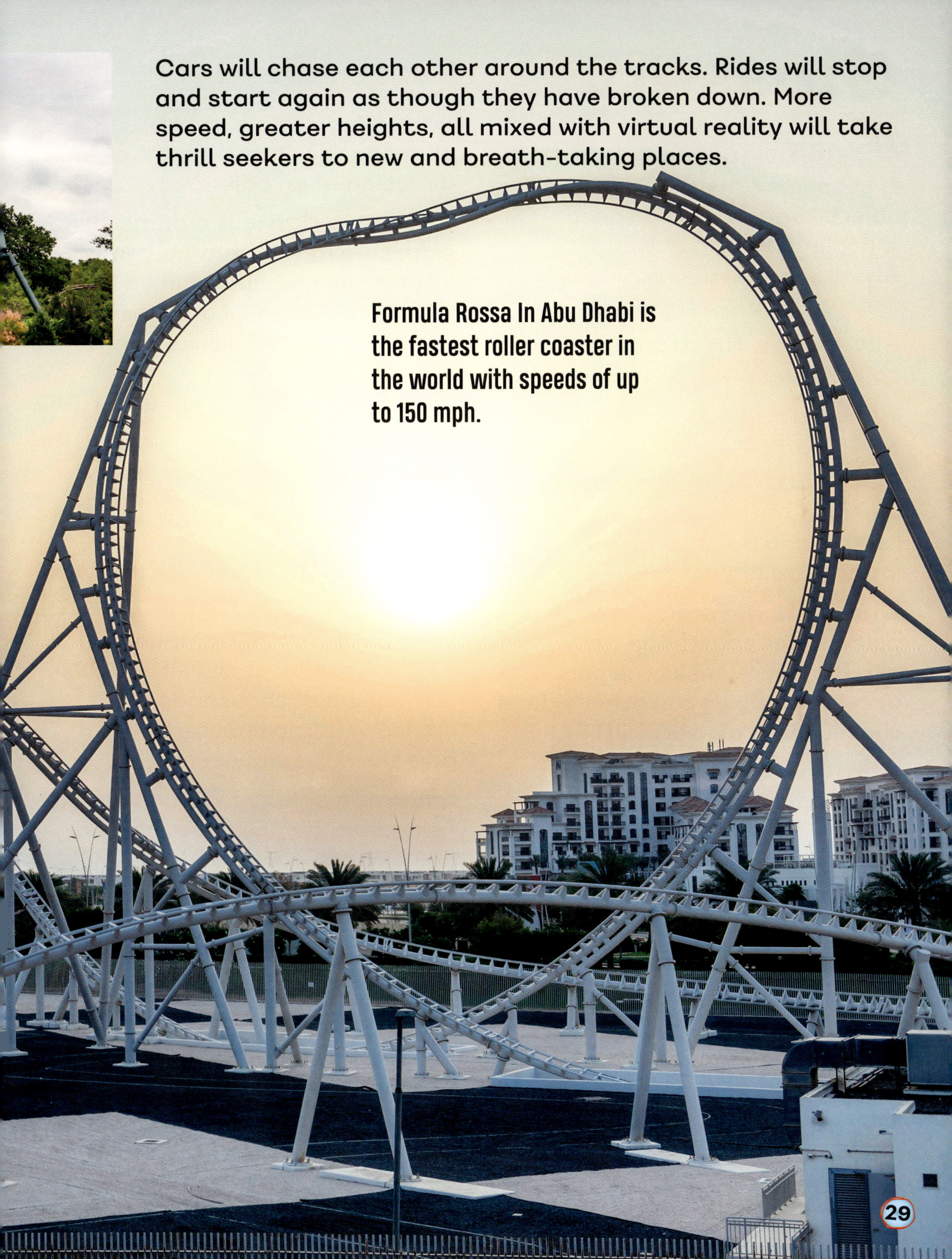

Cars will chase each other around the tracks. Rides will stop and start again as though they have broken down. More speed, greater heights, all mixed with virtual reality will take thrill seekers to new and breath-taking places.

Formula Rossa In Abu Dhabi is the fastest roller coaster in the world with speeds of up to 150 mph.

Glossary

Acceleration is an increase in speed as time passes. An object that is gaining speed is acclerating. An object whose speed is decreasing is decelerating.

Attract means a force that pulls objects together (**see also repel**)

Axle is the central rod around which a wheel turns.

Catapults are devices that launch a roller coaster ride from its starting point to an almost immediate high speed.

Chain lift is a device used to pull a roller coaster up a tall hill. It then releases the cars to accelerate down the other side of the hill. (**see also lift hill**).

Compressed air is air that is pressed into less space. It can be used to propel roller coasters into very fast launches.

Electromagnet is a magnet that produces a powerful magnetic force when electricity flows through it (**see also magnets**).

Energy is the ability to make something happen. There are many forms of energy.

Force is a push or pull that changes the shape, speed, or direction of an object.

Geodesic dome is a dome-like structure made from polygons (many-sided shapes) joined together. Triangles are often used because they are such strong shapes.

Gravity is the force that pulls one mass toward another. Gravity also causes falling objects to accelerate as they fall toward Earth.

Inclined plane is another name for a ramp.

Intricate means complicated. The framework of the Eiffel Tower is made up of thousands of intricate lattice patterns which give the tower its strength.

Lever is a simple machine made from a bar located over a pivot point. When one end of the bar is pushed down, the other end is pushed up.

Lift hill is the first—and usually highest—hill on a roller coaster. The drop from this height helps propel the cars through the rest of the ride.

Magnetic propulsion is powering an object forward using magnets.

Magnets are metals that attract other metals; usually those that contain iron.

Pivot is a point around which an object turns.

Poles are the opposite points on a magnet where the magnetic forces are strongest (**see also magnets**).

Pulley is a simple machine. Rope pulled through a wheel lifts an object at the other end.

Ramp is a simple machine that is a slope raised at one end. Ramps make it easier to move or lower objects.

Repel is to push away or apart. It is the opposite of attract.

Rigid means stiff, unchanging in shape.

Weight is the pull of gravity on an object's mass.

Index

A
Acceleration 8-9, 14-17
Axles 6-8

B
Baron 12-13
Big One, The 20-21

C-D
Catapults 12-13, 16-17
Complex machines 4-7
Compressed air 16-17
Crossbeams 22-25
Disneyland 6-7

E
Eiffel Tower 22-23
Electromagnets 14-15, 28-29
Energy 16-17
Engines 6-7, 12-13

F
Forces 8-11, 16-17, 22-25
Formula Rossa 28-29
Frameworks 18-19, 22-23

G
Geodesic domes 24-25

Gravity 8-9, 12-13

H
Hyperonic XLC 16-17

L
Launch systems 14-17
Levers 4-7, 10-11
Lift hills 12-15

M-N
Machines
  Complex 4-7
  Levers 4-7, 10-11
  Pulleys 4-5, 10-11
  Ramps 4-5, 8-9
  Simple 4-11
  Wheels 4-11
Magnets 14-15, 28-29
Matterhorn Bobsleds 6-7
Nickelodeon Universe 28-29

P
Pivots 10-11
Propulsion 12-17, 28-29
Pulleys 4-5, 10-11

R
Ramps 4-5, 8-9

Red Force 14-16
Roller coasters
  Baron 12-13
  Big One, The 20-21
  Design of 20-27
  Formula Rossa 28-29
  Hyperonic XLC 16-17
  Matterhorn Bobsleds 6-7
  Red Force 14-16
  Steel 6-7, 18-21, 24-25
  Storm Runner 16-17
  Superman 16-17
  Wooden 18-19, 22-23
  X-scream 10-11

S
Seesaws 10-11
Spaceship Earth 24-25
Storm Runner 16-17
Stratosphere Tower 10-11
Superman 16-17

W-X
Weights 10-13, 22-25
Wheels 4-11
Wood 18-19, 22-23
X-scream 10-11

Copyright © 2020 Hungry Tomato Ltd.
First published 2020 by Hungry Tomato Ltd
F1, Old Bakery Studios, Blewetts Wharf, Malpas Road, Truro, Cornwall, TR1 1QH, UK

ISBN 978-1-913077-88-4
Printed and bound in China

A CIP catalogue record for this book is available from the British Library.
No part of this publication may be reproduced, copied, stored in a retrieval system or transmitted in any form or by any means electronic, mechanical, photocopying, recording or otherwise without prior written permission of the copyright owner.

Picture credits
Shutterstock. 1: johnbraid. 2-3: Anton Balazh. 4-5: aleksandr4300, Michele_Arts. 6-7: SIHASAKPRACHUM, gokturk_06. 8-9: MyImages - Micha, Mark stock, Cassiohabib. 10-11: sogood_patrick, BlueRingMedia. 12-13: K13 ART, Rudmer Zwerver 14-15: Pit Stock, SARYMSAKOV ANDREY, udaix. 16-17: SeaRain, Milan Sommer. 18-19: Bill Chizek, Tony Wear. 20-21: aleksandr4300 , Cassiohabib , Arina P Habich, aleksandr4300. 22-23: junrong, Lester Fernandes, James Kirkikis. 24-25: Dustie, Vitaliy Snitovets. 26-27: Oleksii Sidorov, aleksandr4300. 28-29: Photos by D, Valerija Polakovska. ,

Every effort has been made to trace copyright holders, and we apologise in advance for any omissions. We would be pleased to insert the appropriate acknowledgments in any subsequent edition of this publication.

www.hungrytomato.com